VICTORIAN LIFE

VICTORIAN TOYS & GAMES

KATRINA SILIPRANDI

Wayland

VICTORIAN LIFE

A VICTORIAN CHRISTMAS

A VICTORIAN FACTORY

A VICTORIAN HOLIDAY

A VICTORIAN HOSPITAL

A VICTORIAN KITCHEN

A VICTORIAN SCHOOL

A VICTORIAN STREET

A VICTORIAN SUNDAY

A VICTORIAN WORKHOUSE

VICTORIAN CLOTHES

VICTORIAN TOYS AND GAMES

VICTORIAN TRANSPORT

HOW WE LEARN ABOUT THE VICTORIANS

Queen Victoria reigned from 1837 to 1901, a time when Britain went through enormous social and industrial changes. We can learn about the Victorians in various ways. We can still see many of their buildings standing today, and we can look at their documents, maps and artefacts, many of which can be found in museums. Photography, invented during Victoria's reign, gives us a good picture of life in Victorian Britain. In this book you will see what Victorian life was like through some of this historical evidence.

Series design: Pardoe Blacker Ltd
Editors: Sarah Doughty and Katie Orchard
Production controller: Carol Stevens

First published in 1994 by Wayland (Publishers) Ltd,
61 Western Road, Hove, East Sussex BN3 1JD, England

© Copyright 1994 Wayland (Publishers) Ltd

British Library Cataloguing in Publication Data
Siliprandi, Katrina
  Victorian Toys and Games. – (Victorian Life Series)
  I. Title II. Series
  688.70941

ISBN 0 7502 1262 4

Printed and bound in Great Britain by B.P.C. Paulton Books.

Cover picture: A collection of Victorian toys and games.

Picture acknowledgements: The Bridgeman Art Library 7 (Anthony Crane Collection), 17 bottom (Private Collection), 23 (Private Collection), 26 top (Bonhams, London) and bottom (Wolverhampton Art Gallery); Mary Evans Picture Library 4, 5 (bottom), 6 (top), 27; Hulton Deutsch 9 (top), 10, 16, 17 (top); Billie Love 14; National Trust 9 (bottom), 11 (top), 13 (bottom); The Robert Opie Collection 6 (bottom), 11 (bottom), 15 (top), 21 (top), 22 (top); Ann Ronan 6 (top), 8; The Victoria and Albert Museum 5 (top), 15 (bottom), 18, 19 (bottom), 25 (bottom).

Thanks to Norfolk Museums Service for supplying items from their museums on pages 12, 13 (top), 19 (top), 20, 21 (bottom), 22 (bottom), 24, 25 (top) and *cover*.

All commissioned photography by GGS Photo Graphics.

CONTENTS

THE TOY INDUSTRY

When Queen Victoria's reign started in 1837, most toys were made by hand. Toymakers usually worked in their own homes. Toys were expensive and many people could not afford to buy them. Poor children did not usually have any toys that had been made by toymakers. After about 1850, toys began to be made in factories and they became cheaper.

Caleb and his daughter at work.

EARLY VICTORIAN TOYMAKERS

This picture comes from a Victorian book called *The Cricket on the Hearth,* by Charles Dickens. It shows a toymaker called Caleb at work, helped by his blind daughter. The work that was done by Caleb in the story shows us what toymakers made in early Victorian times. We find out that Caleb made many different toys. These included Noah's arks, carts, drums, rocking horses, dolls' houses and horses on wheels.

EARLY TOYS

Many of the toys that were sold in early Victorian Britain were not made in this country. It was easiest to make toys from wood, so wood carvers of forest regions specialized in making toys. Germany was the centre of the toy industry in Europe, producing toys like wooden dolls, jumping jacks, horse and carriages, foot soldiers, birds, animals and little buildings. They were made by workers for companies which sold them to other countries.

A wooden rocking horse.

Children stitching and painting dolls, 1878.

CHILD TOYMAKERS

Many children worked to earn a living. They probably never attended school. Some children worked for as long as seventy hours a week in the potteries where they earned about two shillings (10p) a week. They made toys like earthenware dolls, dolls' tea-sets and money boxes.

A law was passed in 1870 that said all children had to go to school. Many children from poor families, like the ones in this picture, had to go out to work and their parents could not afford school fees. After 1891, most schools became free and more children went to school.

TOY SELLERS

Toys were often sold by pedlars. They travelled with a basket of goods to sell. Other toys were bought at penny bazaars. These were stalls in the street. Everything cost one penny. A Victorian penny was worth much more than a penny today.

In a book called *Time and Again*, the author Helen Thomas describes some of the toys sold at a penny bazaar in the 1880s: '...you could buy little Japanese fans, tiny soft dolls with china heads, hands and feet and a mop of black china curls. A bunch of six slate pencils each wrapped with pretty paper to hold, or a wooden lead pencil with a peephole at the top through which you could see a view of Southport. Fragile coloured glass bangles and packets of gay beads to thread.'

A pedlar showing all the toys that he has for sale.

A toy made in a factory by Lehmanns in Germany.

FACTORY-MADE TOYS

From the 1850s, more and more toys were made in factories. Steam power could be used to drive factory machines, which meant that many toys could be made quickly and more cheaply than by hand. Toymaking firms grew up in Germany, France, the USA and Britain. The growth of railways meant that toys could be distributed very quickly from the factory to shops all around the country.

TOYSHOPS

This is a picture of the Lowther Arcade in London, an area where there were many shops selling toys. There were similar arcades in other towns. In Victorian times, not all toys were sold in toyshops.

Victorian opticians not only sold spectacles but also items like telescopes, microscopes and scientific toys. Some optical toys (that played tricks with the eye) were sold by opticians.

The Lowther Arcade in London.

PLAYTIME

Do you play with your toys when you come home from school? In Victorian Britain many poor children had less time for playing than children have today, especially if they worked and did not go to school. Even for children who attended school, some had no time to play with toys. They helped their parents with jobs like cutting wood, fetching water and looking after younger brothers and sisters.

Playing cricket in the street.

STREET GAMES

Poor people's homes in towns were often very crowded and did not have gardens. The children had to play in the street. The streets were quieter and safer than they are today. Horse-drawn carriages were the main type of transport on the roads.

PLAYING OUTSIDE

The boys in this picture are leap-frogging. This was a favourite outdoor game. Recalling his Victorian childhood, a writer called Taffy Lewis wrote: 'As the seasons changed so did our games...as you were going to school you'd see eight to ten boys leap-frogging, one over the other until they reached the school.'

Other games that children enjoyed playing outside were simple games like marbles and conkers.

Leap-frogging, 1857.

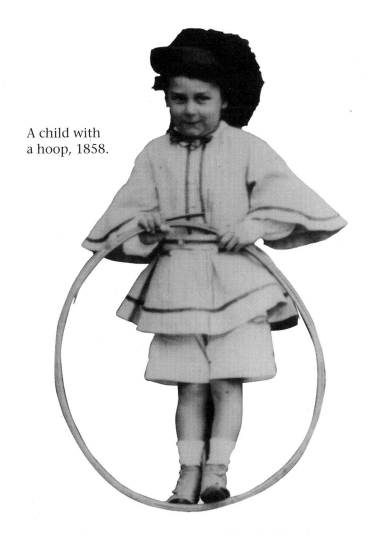

A child with a hoop, 1858.

Both rich and poor children liked to play with hoops. A child used a stick to push the hoop along. In the country, the village blacksmith often made iron hoops. Spinning tops were also popular. They were cheap, easy to carry and could be spun anywhere that was flat. In a book about his own childhood, Edward Thomas, a poet, wrote: 'Going home we spun our tops or two of us helped ourselves along by bowling hoops.'

STREET DANCING

These children are dancing in the street. They are using a lamp-post as a maypole. Hopscotch and skipping were other popular games. Children often used an old piece of clothesline for a skipping-rope. Here is a Scottish skipping rhyme from Victorian times:

'Waan toe three,
Ma mammy caught a flea;
She saltit it an' peppered it
An pit it in her tea.'

This skipping rhyme comes from Wales:

'Eaver Weaver, chimney sweeper,
Had a wife and couldn't keep her,
Had another, didn't love her,
Up the chimney he did shove her'.

Children playing in slums, 1892.

THE NURSERY

Rich Victorian children often had their own room to sleep, eat and play in, called a nursery. The picture on the next page shows what a nursery was like in late Victorian times. The nursery was usually at the top of the house. There was a guard around the fire to keep the children safe. Rich children were looked after by their own servants. From about 1870 it was usual for rich children to spend only an hour with their parents every day, usually after tea.

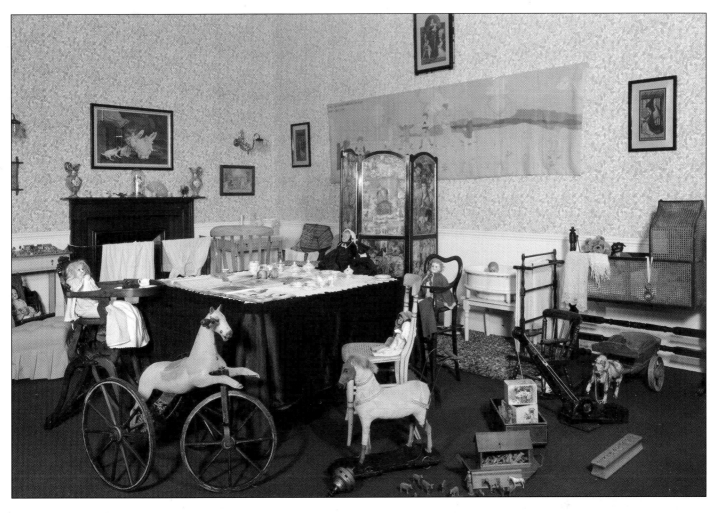

The nursery at Wallington.

SUNDAY GAMES

In some Victorian homes, children were not allowed to play with most of their toys on a Sunday. This was because Sunday was the day to go to church and Sunday school. The rest of the day was spent reading the Bible and thinking about God and Jesus. One of the few toys children could play with on a Sunday was their Noah's ark because the story of Noah is in the Bible.

A Noah's ark toy.

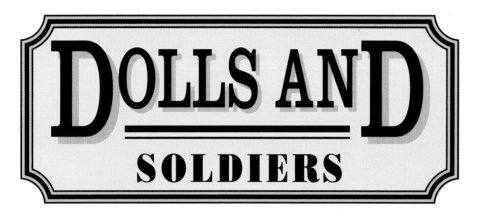

DOLLS AND SOLDIERS

Playing is fun, but when we play we also learn about how the world works. Sometimes we need things to help our imagination when we are playing. Toys become almost real. In Victorian times it was thought that playing with toys like dolls and soldiers would help children to understand about people. Children could learn how adults behaved from playing with these toys.

DOLLS' TEA PARTY

The tea-set in this picture is made from china. The children who played with it had to be careful not to break it. Many Victorian dolls were also breakable, as their heads were often

A china tea-set.

made from wax or china. Some dolls had heads made from papier mâché covered in a thin layer of wax. The dolls' bodies were made from stuffed kid or calico. Their eyes were made from glass. Baby dolls first appeared in the 1850s.

DOLLS

These dolls would have been owned by rich children. When they were first made, they would have been sold unclothed. Clothes were specially made for each doll, perhaps by a doll's dressmaker or by the owner's mother. Many dolls' clothes were beautifully made with tiny hand stitches. Poorer children probably had rag dolls to play with. Other soft toys, like lambs and ducks, were not made until later Victorian times.

A selection of dolls.

DOLLS' HOUSES

A Victorian child might have had a doll's house like this in the nursery. Originally, dolls' houses were made for middle-class families to help girls to learn about home-making. Many Victorian dolls' houses were made for the children of rich parents.

Dolls' houses can show us what rich homes in Victorian times were like. In this doll's house you can see seven of the rooms, including the attic, and the dining-room where the table is laid for a meal.

Inside a doll's house.

THE BABY CARRIAGE

Prams were called perambulators in Victorian times. The most common early Victorian perambulators were three-wheeled pushchairs in which the child sat. In the 1880s the baby carriage appeared. This was a perambulator in which a child could lie down. Most families could not afford to buy a pram for their babies, and in London parents were able to hire prams to use. The baby carriage in the picture is a child's toy and is much smaller than a real pram would have been.

A child's baby carriage, 1899.

A SET OF FLATS

Toy soldiers like these are called flats because they are less than one millimetre thick. They were very popular in Victorian times. Most flats were made in Germany. They were made in moulds from lead or tin. Full rounded figures were sometimes made in solid metal, but they were much heavier and more expensive than flats.

Flat soldiers made in Germany.

Rounded, die-cast solders.

SOLDIERS

In 1893 a British toymaker called William Britain invented a new way of making toy soldiers. He made hollow, rounded figures like the ones above. As they were hollow, they were lighter than solid metal ones.

A worker could make 300 figures an hour from a hand-held mould. These soldiers were very popular. In 1900, Britain's soldiers were sold in sets for 5p a set. The firm called Britains is still making and selling toys today.

TOYS THAT
MOVE

Do you have some toys that need batteries to work? Victorian children liked to play with toys that moved, but batteries like the ones we use today had not been invented. Children had to push or pull toys to make them move. Other toys used clockwork or stretched elastic bands to make them work.

TOYS WITH WHEELS

Toys like the one in this picture copied real forms of transport. Toys were made to look just like trains, motor cars, bicycles and boats. Such toys were widely produced by German firms. They can usually be identified today because they have the maker's mark on them. Marklin, Rock and Graner, and Lehmann were all famous German toymakers.

A child and mother with a wheeled toy.

ROCKING HORSE

The boy in this picture is riding a rocking horse made from wood. The hooves are fixed to long, curved rockers. In 1880 a rocking horse with a frame was invented. Victorian children also enjoyed playing with wooden horses on wheels that could be pushed or pulled along. The hobby-horse was another popular toy. This was a carved horse's head on a stick that children could pretend to ride.

A boy and girl with a rocking horse, 1865.

CLOCKWORK DANCING FIGURES

Toys like this are called automata. When they are wound up, they move like real people. These dancing figures were made in the USA in about 1865.

US toymakers usually made simple automata like this that would appeal to children. In Europe some toys were made for adults but they were very expensive. Sometimes the toys not only played music but moved as well. Britains was one of the few British firms to make automata.

Automata, 1860–70.

MECHANICAL TRAINS

This mechanical train is made from tin plate. Many Victorian tin plate toys sold in Britain from the 1860s were made in Nuremberg, Germany. In just ten years the Germans built over 240 factories, eventually employing over 1,000 people.

The toys were made by stamping out parts from sheets of tin plate. Steam presses were used from 1850. At the end of Queen Victoria's reign, some factories were powered by electricity. But the detail on the toys was still usually painted by hand. In 1850, a tin plate train with two carriages cost 15p (this was a whole day's wages for many working people). Only richer children could have owned such a train. By 1890 many small tin plate toys could be bought from street sellers for less than 1p.

A mechanical train.

OPTICAL TOYS

In 1824 a French man named Roget discovered what he called 'persistence of vision'. This meant that a person could watch a number of images, one after the other, from a single point, and it looked as if the images were moving. This led to the invention of toys like the zoetrope. The zoetrope was a metal drum with slits cut in it. A series of pictures was drawn on a strip of paper called a shut. The shut was put into the drum. When the drum was spun around it looked as though the figure on the shut was running.

A zoetrope, developed in 1834.

MAGIC LANTERN

This is a magic lantern. Pictures were painted on glass slides and projected on to a screen by the lantern. In Victorian times, moving pictures could be made by having separate pieces of glass bound into the hand-painted slides. Moving picture toys led to the invention of the cinema in the 1890s.

A magic lantern and glass slides.

Many Victorian toys were made to help children with their education. Rich children had cards and bricks with letters of the alphabet and numbers on them. These were to help the children with reading and sums. There were toys to teach history, geography, Bible stories and how things worked.

PICTURE BLOCKS

These wooden story blocks were made in 1881. They could be piled up on top of each other to teach simple building skills or they could be used to teach reading. The story of the marriage of Jenny Wren and the death of Cock Robin is told in verse on the top of the eight largest blocks. The pictures around the sides go with the story. The blocks fit inside each other.

Story blocks.

WOODEN BUILDING BRICKS

Blocks like these could be used to make models of many different buildings. This set included pictures for the child to copy. In early Victorian times the blocks were usually made from wood. Many of them came to Britain from Germany. They were sold by opticians because they were seen as scientific toys. In 1870 an advertisement for E. Lapuis, an optician, offered 'building slabs for boys'.

Wooden blocks with a picture book.

'STONE' BLOCKS

In 1880 an Austrian called Dr Richter invented blocks that were made from sand and chalk and came in different colours. These looked much more realistic than wooden blocks. They were first made in Britain in 1882. Buildings over one metre high could be made with the more expensive sets. In Victorian times you could buy cards printed with pictures of parts of buildings. These could be clipped together to make models that really looked like houses and churches.

A set of blocks made from sand and chalk.

MECCANO

Meccano was invented by Frank Hornby at the end of Queen Victoria's reign. It was an exciting new toy because it could be used to make mechanical models. Hornby made the first set from copper strips for his two sons. The metal strips had holes in them. They were joined together using nuts and bolts. Meccano sets included steel rods and wheels so carts, wagons and cranes could be built with them. The first sets of Meccano were sold in 1901. They were packed in tin boxes and cost $37\frac{1}{2}$ p. At this time Meccano was called Mechanics Made Easy.

A Meccano box.

JIGSAWS

A variety of jigsaws.

Jigsaws like those opposite were called 'dissected' (cut up) puzzles in Victorian times. The puzzles and their boxes were made from wood. In the first part of Queen Victoria's reign they were hand-coloured. The puzzles often included facts for children to learn. Later puzzles were often just pictures to piece together. Queen Victoria enjoyed jigsaws. In the evening she sometimes got the Prime Minister and the Lord Chamberlain to help her to piece together her jigsaws.

Victorian picture bricks.

PICTURE BRICKS

Picture bricks had a part of a picture on each side. This meant that six pictures could be made from a set like this. Early Victorian sets were hand-coloured. They were made from wood. They came in wooden boxes with sliding lids. Victorian children also had puzzles made of different shapes. They used them to make patterns called mosaics.

BOARD
& CARD GAMES

Do you enjoy playing games like snakes and ladders? Games like this are called board games. Television and computers had not been invented, so Victorian children and their parents played board games together at home more often than most families do today. Victorian families who could afford them had many board games. Some of the games they played have been handed down to us.

RACE GAMES

Race games were the most popular board games among children. Players threw a die and then moved counters around the board on a marked path. The first player to reach the end of the path was the winner. Sometimes the player was allowed another turn; sometimes he or she had to go back and try again. Some Victorian race games were made to teach children about geography, history or religion. Other games helped children to learn about how to behave.

Popular board games.

TEETOTUMS

Teetotums were six-sided or eight-sided spinners. A teetotum like this was often used instead of a die for playing race games. Many Victorians thought dice should not be used because they were used in gambling. Teetotums and dice were usually made from bone or ivory.

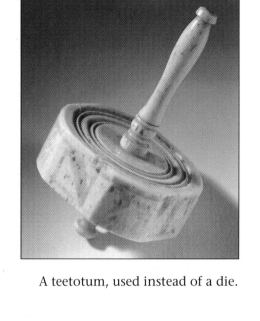

A teetotum, used instead of a die.

HAPPY FAMILIES

Here are some cards from a Victorian pack for playing Happy Families. Players had to collect sets of cards. Each set had four family members–mother, father, son and daughter. Quartets was another popular card game in Victorian Britain. The game was made to help children learn facts about composers, writers, history and geography. The idea of this game was also to collect sets of cards (four of a kind). Sometimes children made their own cards for playing quartets.

Cards from a set of Happy Families.

CHESS

The adults in this painting are playing chess. Rich Victorian families had games tables to play on, like the one in the picture. The board is built into the table. The table could also be used for draughts. Chess was a popular game in many countries in Victorian times. Henry Staunton became the first world chess champion in 1843. Victorian boys from rich families learnt to play chess at public school. Adults also liked to play backgammon and solitaire.

Playing chess.

PLAYING CARDS

In this Victorian painting the adults are playing a card game. In about 1870, Thomas De La Rue, a manufacturer, introduced playing cards with rounded corners and numbers on them. The pictures of the king, queen and jack on the backs of the cards remained the same as 300 years before, except that it became usual for cards to have two heads, one at the top, and one at the bottom.

Adults playing a card game.

VICTORIAN CHRISTMAS

This picture is from the cover of a Victorian book. Rich children had many toys and at Christmas time they were given presents. By the end of Queen Victoria's reign, many toys could be bought more cheaply than in the early 1800s because they were made in factories. But most poor children still had very few toys and games. They made their own toys from paper, cardboard boxes, acorns and conkers. These toys have not survived. Most of the toys and games you see preserved in museums belonged to children from rich families.

Father Christmas delivering presents on a Victorian Christmas card.

TIME LINE

BC	AD 0		500		
		43	410		
			'THE DARK AGES'		
CELTS		ROMAN BRITAIN	ANGLO-SAXONS		VIKINGS

LATE 1700s

1778 Lotto, a similar game to bingo introduced.

EARLY 1800s

1824 P. M. Roget investigated 'persistence of vision'.

1830s

1837 Queen Victoria's reign started.

1840s

1843 First world chess champion, Howard Staunton.

1846 Marble scissors invented. This meant that glass marbles could be made more quickly than before.

1850s

Toys first made from Indiarubber.

Steam power introduced in some German toy factories.

1851 Great Exhibition, London. Tin plate toys from Germany were shown for the first time and toys were now made in factories.

1066 — MIDDLE AGES — **1485** **1603** **1714** **1837** **1901**

NORMANS   TUDORS   STUARTS   GEORGIANS   VICTORIANS   20TH CENTURY

1870s

Clay marbles manufactured.

Dolls' heads made from porcelain.

1870 Celluloid invented.

De La Rue introduced rounded corners on playing cards.

1876 Ludo first played in Britain.

1880s

Introduction of baby carriages.

1880 Ernst Lehmann introduced coil-spring clockwork.

First manufactured soft toys made by Steiff firm.

Framed rocking horse invented.

1885 Slazenger firm started

1888 The game Othello invented.

1889 Tiddlywinks invented.

1890s

First machines for making marbles invented.

First toy cars made.

1893 First electric toy train made.

William Britain invented process to make hollow, fully rounded toy soldiers.

1897 Chad Valley toy firm started.

1900s

1901 Mechanics Made Easy (Meccano) first sold by Frank Hornby.

Queen Victoria died.

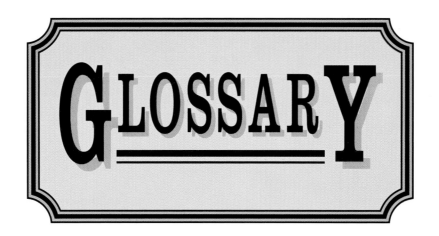

GLOSSARY

Automata   Mechanical toys that move.

Backgammon   A game played by two players on a board with dice and counters.

Calico   Plain white or cream cotton cloth.

Composer   A person who writes new music.

Dissected   When something is taken apart or cut up into pieces.

Earthenware   Plates and bowls made from baked clay.

Gambling   Playing a game in order to win money.

Ivory   Hard white material made from the tusks of elephants, walruses and hippopotami.

Kid   Leather made from goatskin.

Mechanical   When something is worked or done by machinery.

Mosaic   A piece of work made up of small shapes that fit together to make a pattern.

Optician   A person who sells instruments to do with sight, eyes and the science of light.

'Persistence of vision'   If an object is seen in a quick series of closely similar positions, one after the other, it gives the impression of a single, moving image.

Solitaire   A game played by one person with a board and either with balls or marbles.

Tin plate   Thin sheet of either iron or steel, coated with tin.

BOOKS TO READ

For older readers:

Bethnal Green Museum of Childhood Guide Book (Victoria and Albert Museum, 1986) Available from the Victoria and Albert Museum.

For children:

Blanchard, H. *Toys and Games* series (Wayland, 1992)

Royston, A. *What's Inside? Toys* (Dorling Kindersley, 1991)

Tanner, G. & Wood, T. *Toys* (A & C Black, 1993)

Thomson, R. *Toys and Games* (Franklin Watts, 1992)

Williams, J. *Toys* (Wayland, 1993)

PLACES TO VISIT

Many museums have displays of old toys and games. Some also have reconstructed Victorian nurseries. Here are just a few of them:

ENGLAND

Bedfordshire: Luton Museum and Art Gallery, Wardown Park, Luton LU2 7HA. Tel: 0582 369412

Derbyshire: Museum of Childhood, Sudbury Hall, Sudbury DE6 5HT. Tel: 028 378305

London: Bethnal Green Museum of Childhood, Cambridge Heath Road, London E2 9PA. Tel: 081 980 4315

London Toy and Model Museum, 23 Craven Hill, W2 3EN. Tel: 071 262 7905 or 9450

Pollock's Toy Museum, 1 Scala Street, London W1P 1LT. Tel: 071 636 334524

Norfolk: Strangers' Hall Museum, Charing Cross, Norwich NR2 4AL. Tel: 0603 667229

Worcestershire: Hereford and Worcester County Museum, Hartlebury Castle, Hartlebury, near Kidderminster DY11 7XZ. Tel: 0299 250416

Yorkshire: York Castle Museum, Tower Street, York YO1 1RY. Tel: 0904 653611

SCOTLAND

Lothian: Museum of Childhood, High Street, Edinburgh. Tel: 031 225 1131

WALES

Gwynned: Museum of Childhood, Menoir Bridge, Anglesey. Tel: 0248 712 498

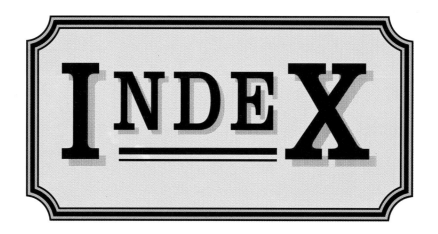

INDEX